COLOUR MY
CANADA

ELINA DIAZ

ISBN 978-1-63353-456-8

Canada is the second largest country in the world by total land area (Russia is the largest).

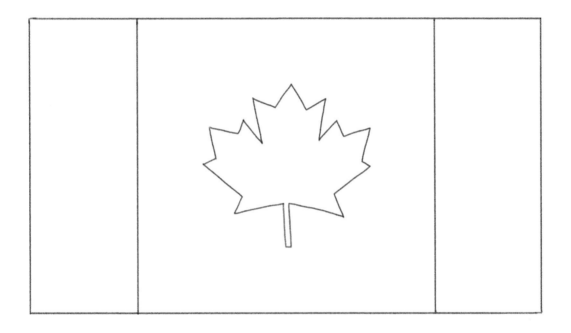

The maple leaf has been a Canadian symbol since the
1800's, but it's use in the current Canadian flag
only dates back to 1965.

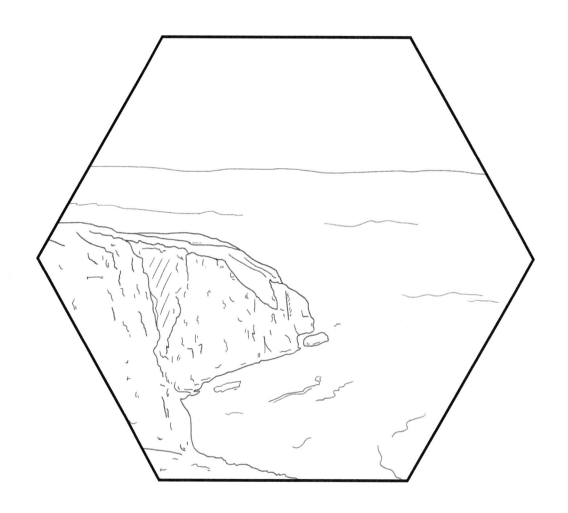

Canada features the longest coastline in the world,
stretching 202,080 kilometres (125,570 miles).

The name Canada comes from the word 'kanata' which
means 'settlement' or 'village' in the language of the
indigenous Saint Lawrence Iroquoians.

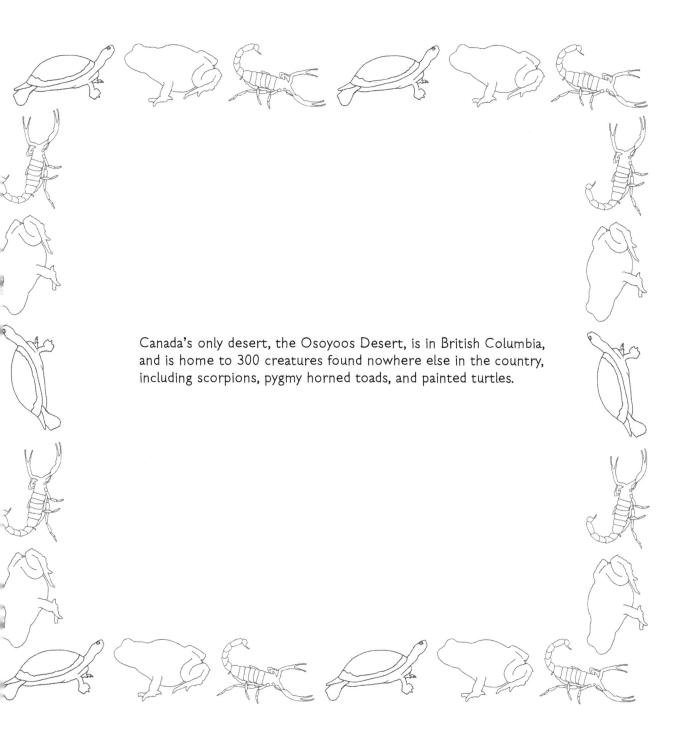

Canada's only desert, the Osoyoos Desert, is in British Columbia, and is home to 300 creatures found nowhere else in the country, including scorpions, pygmy horned toads, and painted turtles.

Canada has more lakes than the rest of world combined.

Basketball was invented by a Canadian,
James Naismith, in 1891.

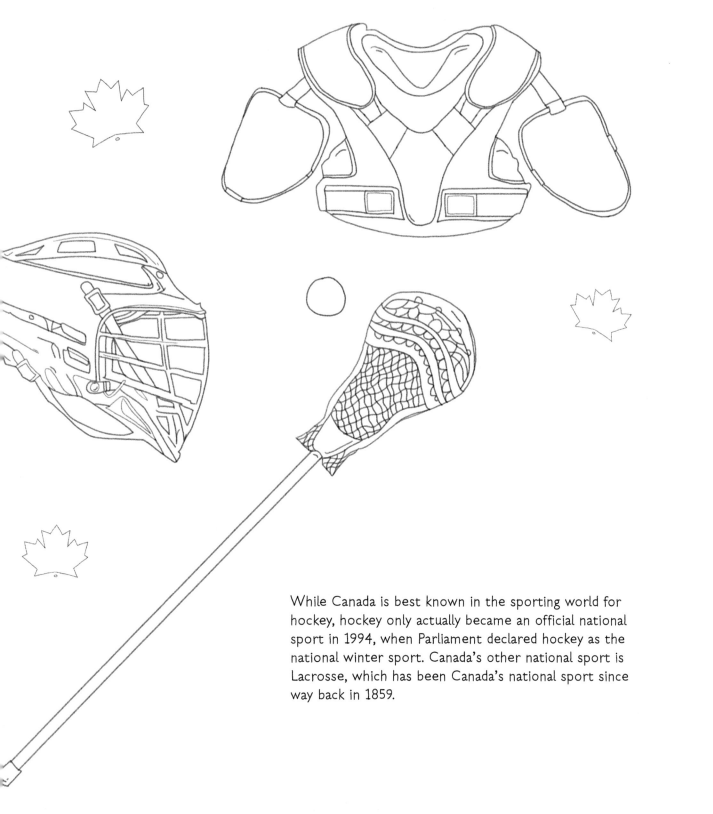

While Canada is best known in the sporting world for hockey, hockey only actually became an official national sport in 1994, when Parliament declared hockey as the national winter sport. Canada's other national sport is Lacrosse, which has been Canada's national sport since way back in 1859.

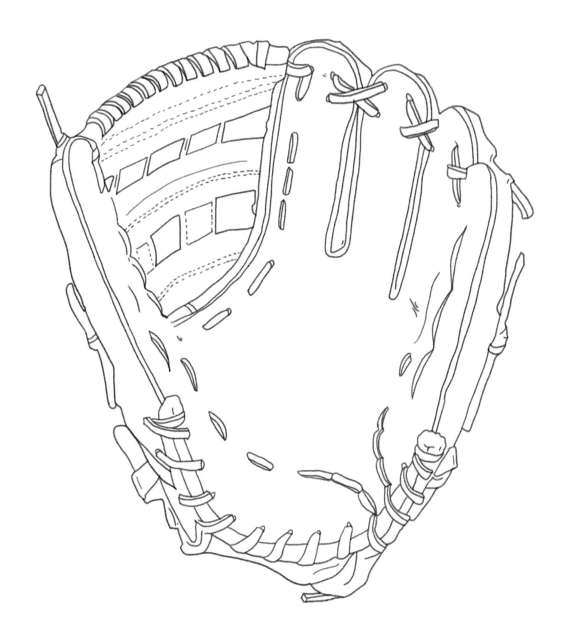

The baseball glove was invented in Canada in 1883.

No cows in Canada are given artificial hormones for milk production.

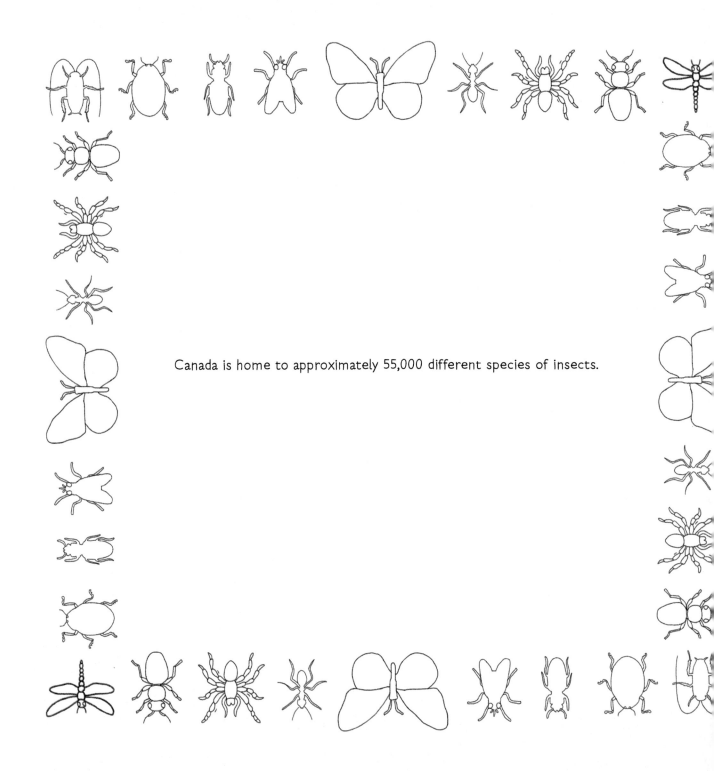

Canada is home to approximately 55,000 different species of insects.

Wasaga Beach in Ontario is the longest fresh water beach in the world.

Princess Juliana of the Dutch Royal family, along with her children, was sheltered in Canada for three years while the Nazis were occupying the Netherlands. And for one day in 1943, Ottawa designated a hospital room to be "extraterritorial" (international) ground so a Dutch princess could be born a full Dutch citizen.

To show her gratitude, Princess Juliana sent 100,000 tulip bulbs to Canada, and every year to this day, the Netherlands sends Canada 10,000 tulip bulbs, inspiring Ottawa's annual Tulip Festival.

Half of Canada is covered with forests, which should come as no surprise considering 10% of the world's forests are here.

Canada has the world's smallest jail – in Rodney, Ontario;
it's only 24.3 square meters (270 square feet).

BEATLEMANIA

Sandy Gardiner, a journalist with the Ottawa Journal in the '60s, coined the term 'Beatlemania' while he was writing a story about the Beatles.

Cheddar is the most popular cheese in Canada. On average Canadians consume 23.4 pounds per person annually.

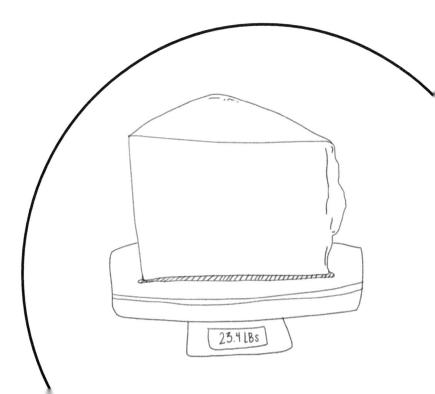

23.4 LBs

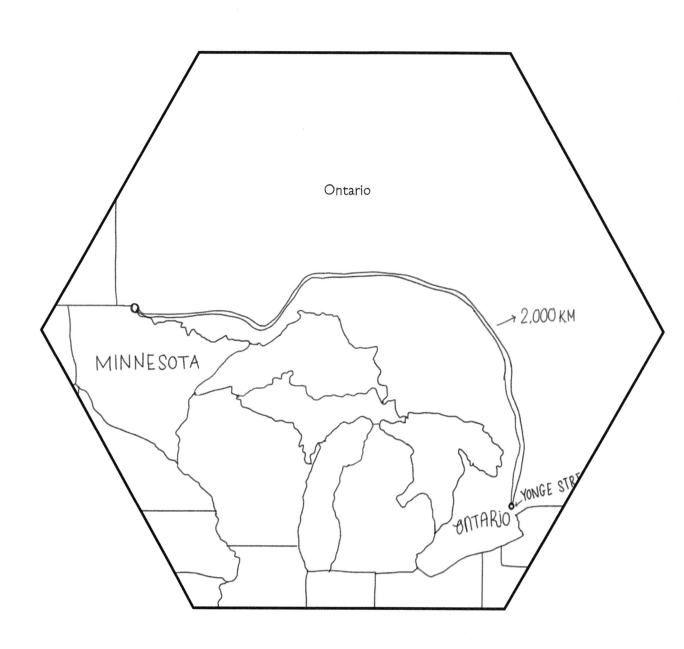

Ontario

MINNESOTA

→ 2,000 KM

ONTARIO

YONGE STR

Canada is home to the longest street in the world. Yonge Street in Ontario starts at Lake Ontario, and runs north through Ontario to the Minnesota border, a distance of almost 2,000 km.

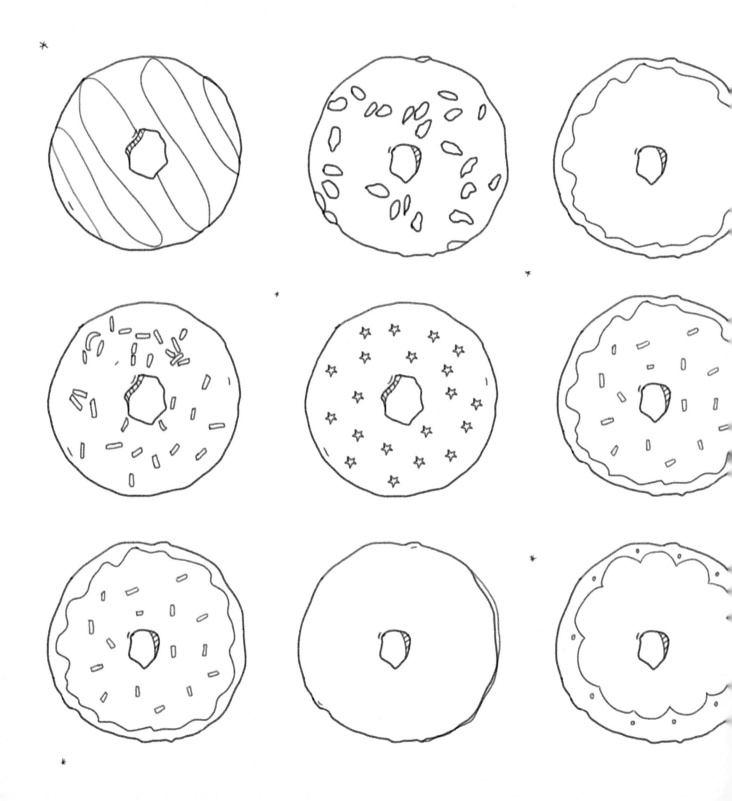

There are more doughnut shops in Canada per capita
than any other country – Yum!

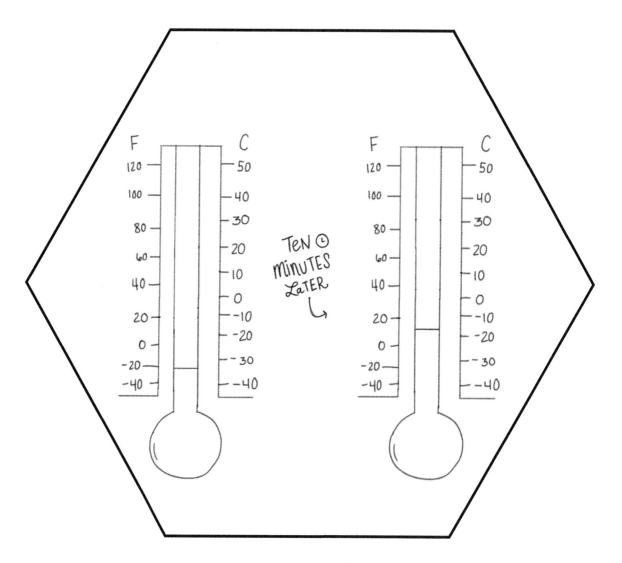

Calgary is famous for its Chinooks – a weather phenomenon that can raise the temperature by 10 degrees in a matter of minutes.

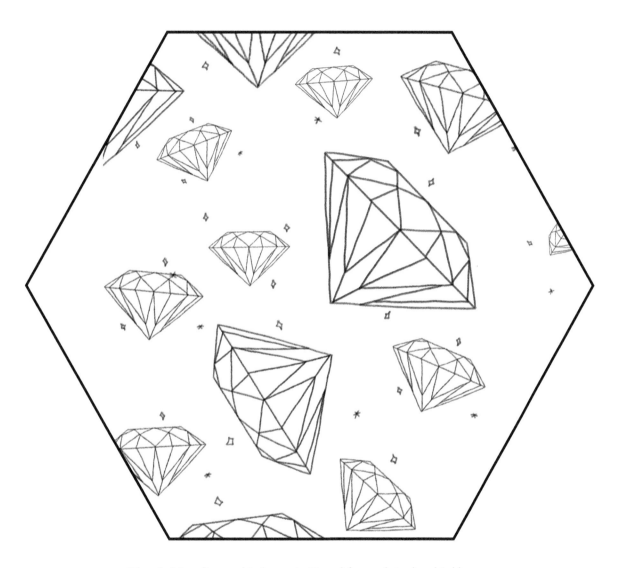

The thriving diamond industry in Canada's north is the third largest diamond producer in the world.

Superman was co-created by Canadian Joe Shuster and American Jerry Siegel, and the fictional city of Metropolis is based on the city of Toronto.

A large part of Canada, including Hudson Bay and surrounding areas, actually has less gravity than the rest of the planet.

The average Canadian buys 76 litres of beer per year.

BONJOUR
Merci OUI
NON

Montreal is the world's second-largest
French speaking city after Paris.

Fifty percent of the world's polar bears live in the Canadian territory of Nunavut.

A bear cub named Winnipeg was exported from Canada to the London Zoo in 1915. A little boy named Christopher Robin Milne loved to visit Winnipeg, or Winnie for short. His love for the bear cub inspired the stories written by his father, A.A. Milne, about Winnie-the-Pooh.

Canada has six time zones.

About 90% of Canada's population is concentrated within 160 kilometers (100 miles) of the Canada/US border.

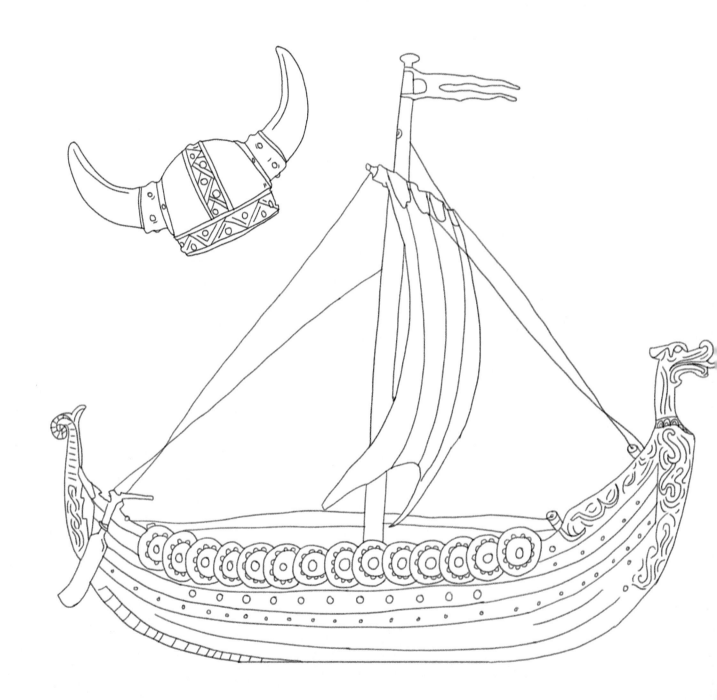

The east coast of Canada was settled by Vikings in approximately 1000 AD.
Sorry Columbus! It's definitely worth a visit to L'Anse aux Meadows.

You can swim with beluga whales in Churchill, Manitoba.

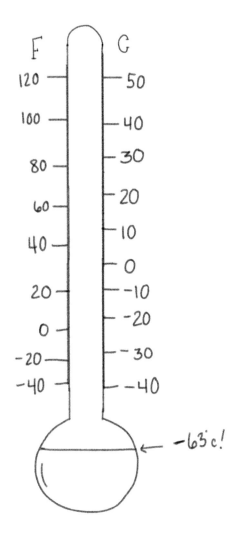

The coldest temperature ever recorded in Canada was -63C (-81.4F) on February 3, 1957 in Snag, Yukon.

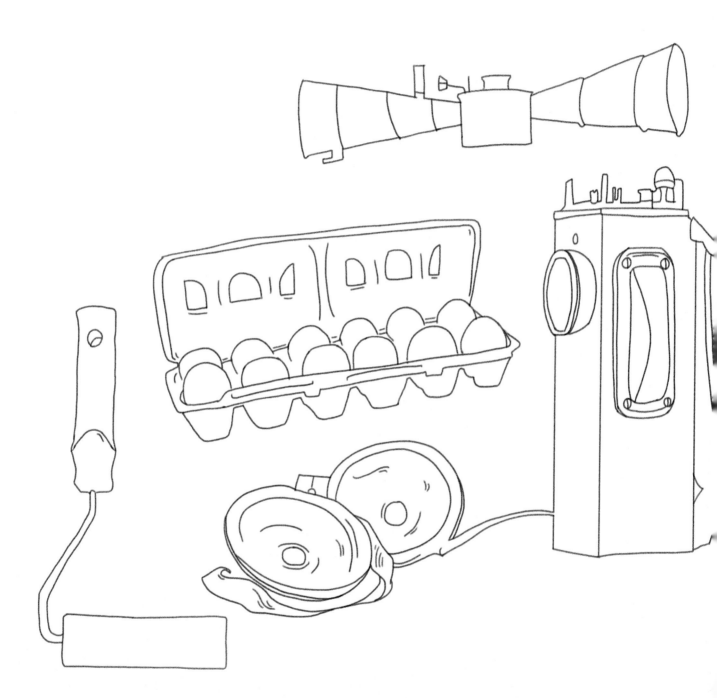

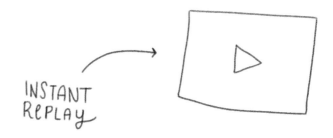

INSTANT REPLAY

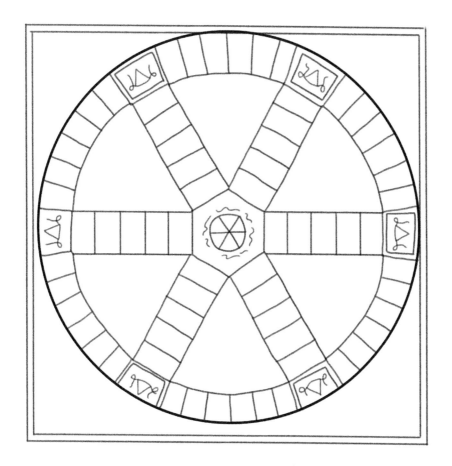

IMAX

Things that were invented by Canadians:

Trivial Pursuit, IMAX, walkie-talkies, instant replay, paint rollers, egg cartons, and foghorns.

The average life expectancy at birth is 81.16 years –
the sixth highest in the world.

John Cabot was the first explorer to reach Canada in 1497.

In Banff National Park, Alberta, overpasses were created just for wildlife, so they can pass over highways safely. The wildlife that uses the overpasses include bears, wolves, moose, cougars, coyotes, bighorn sheep, to name just a few.

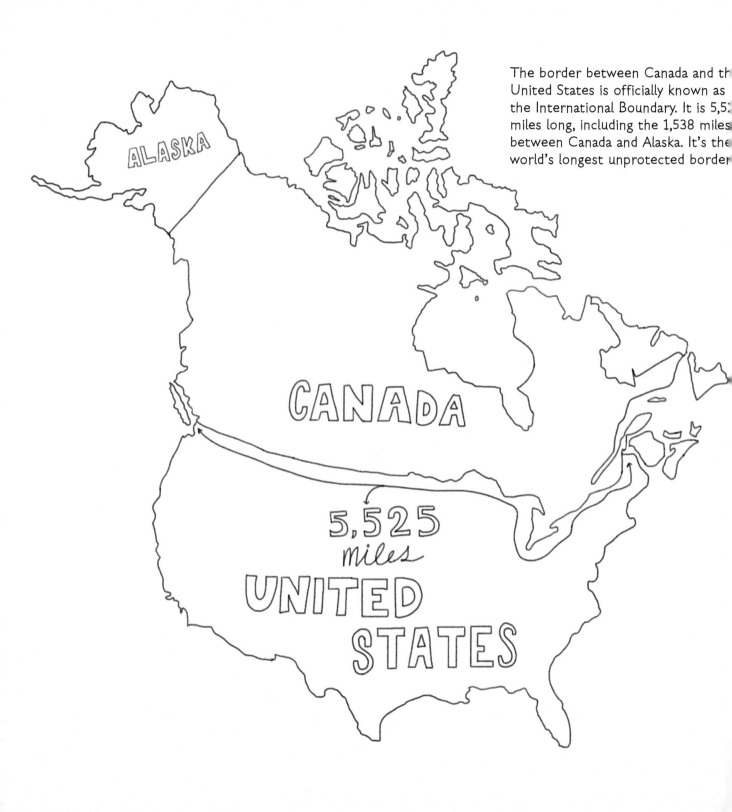

ALASKA

The border between Canada and th
United States is officially known as
the International Boundary. It is 5,5
miles long, including the 1,538 miles
between Canada and Alaska. It's the
world's longest unprotected border

CANADA

5,525
miles

UNITED
STATES

Common contenders for Canada's national food include poutine, maple syrup, & butter tarts.

Wine is produced in British Columbia, Ontario, Québec and Nova Scotia.

Greenpeace was founded in Vancouver in 1971.
The environmental organization now has offices
in over 40 countries worldwide.

The Vancouver Polar Bear Swim Club is one of the largest and oldest Polar Bear Clubs in the world. Each New Year's Day since 1920, residents have plunged into the frigid waters of English Bay.

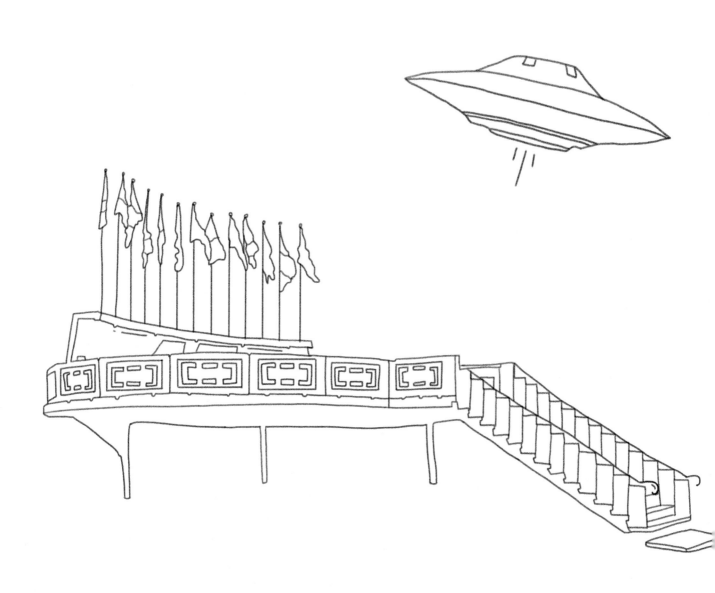

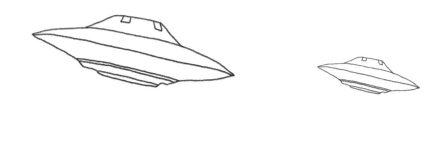

Canada was the first country to build a UFO landing pad. It was built in 1967 in St. Paul, Alberta, and the Minister of National Defence at the time attended the grand opening.

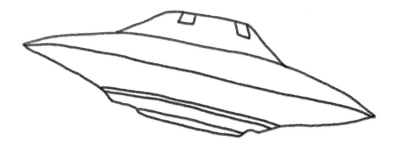

Villages Vacances Valcartier, Québec is the largest winter playground in North America. It has 35 snow slides, skating trails, 5,000 inner tubes and 17 lifts.

EVEREST

Toronto is the 4th most populous city in North America, and is recognized as one of the most multicultural cities in the world.

The city of Toronto started off as York, the capital of Upper Canada in 1793. York was incorporated and renamed Toronto in 1834.

Toronto is North America's third largest venue for movie production.
There are over 25,000 jobs in feature film production.

Fairmont Le Château Frontenac (Québec City), the most
photographed hotel in the world, has been open since 1893.

CPSIA information can be obtained
at www.ICGtesting.com
Printed in the USA
BVOW07s0027300916
463486BV00009B/41/P

9 781633 535